D1689379

Bible Devotions
for Bedtime

Daniel Partner
Illustrated by Richard Hoit

BARBOUR
PUBLISHING

© 2004 by Barbour Publishing, Inc.

All rights reserved. No part of this publication may be reproduced or transmitted for commercial purposes, except for brief quotations in printed reviews, without written permission of the publisher.

Churches and other noncommercial interests may reproduce portions of this book without the express written permission of Barbour Publishing, provided that the text does not exceed 500 words or 5 percent of the entire book, whichever is less and that the text is not material quoted from another publisher. When reproducing text from this book, include the following credit line: "From *Bible Devotions for Bedtime*, published by Barbour Publishing, Inc. Used by permission."

All scripture quotations, unless otherwise noted, are taken from the *Holy Bible*. New Living Translation copyright© 1996, 2004, 2007 by Tyndale House Foundation. Used by permission of Tyndale House Publishers, Inc. Carol Stream, Illinois 60188. All rights reserved.

Scripture quotations marked NIV are taken from the HOLY BIBLE, NEW INTERNATIONAL VERSION®. NIV®. Copyright © 1973, 1978, 1984, 2011 by Biblica, Inc.™ Used by permission. All rights reserved worldwide.

Cover and interior illustrations by Richard Hoit

Published by Barbour Publishing, Inc., P.O. Box 719, Uhrichsville, Ohio 44683, www.barbourbooks.com

Our mission is to publish and distribute inspirational products offering exceptional value and biblical encouragement to the masses.

ecpa Member of the Evangelical Christian Publishers Association

Printed in China.

Jesus said, "Let the little children come to me, and do not hinder them, for the kingdom of heaven belongs to such as these."

MATTHEW 19:14 NIV

"God Rested"

On the seventh day God had finished his work of creation, so he rested from all his work.

GENESIS 2:2

The Bible tells about God's power. And God is strong, too. But God is much more than powerful and strong. God is also holy, eternal, faithful, wise, true, and good. God is light. God is love. God is so much that there are not enough words to tell it all!

The Bible is the book that tells us all we need to know about God. The first thing it says is that God is the Creator, and it tells the story of Creation. And there are not just six days in the Creation story. It took God seven days to finish making everything. The first six days were for working. Then on the seventh day, God rested from all His work. First, God worked to create everything. What is the second thing the Bible tells about God? It says that God rested. But God is so strong and powerful. Why would He need to rest? Maybe to help us remember that we should take time to rest, too!

Dear God, thank You for being who You are—powerful, holy, and full of love. Amen.

"I am giving you a sign."

And God said, "I am giving you a sign. . . .
I have placed my rainbow in the clouds. . . .
Never again will the floodwaters destroy all life."
Genesis 9:12–13, 15

Do you like to see a rainbow in the sky? They are so beautiful! Do you know what makes a rainbow? Sun shining through falling rain. But in Noah's time, there had never been a rainbow before. The rains that brought the flood were the first rains ever. When Noah saw the rains ending, the sun came out. Then Noah and his family saw the very first rainbow ever, and they knew they had survived the Great Flood.

Imagine what Noah's family felt the next time rain clouds came. They must have been afraid of the rain. After all, the first time it rained, the flood destroyed the whole earth! But God didn't want them to be afraid. God promised Noah and his family that He would never again destroy the earth with a flood.

Rainbows are a reminder that this promise is true. God has kept this promise to Noah. Since the time of Noah, floods have never destroyed the whole earth. Remember this whenever you see a rainbow.

The Bible tells many of God's promises.

All these are as real and beautiful as a rainbow. And all of them are true!

Dear God, thank You for always keeping Your word! Amen.

"...with all his might."

Samson put his hands on the two center pillars that held up the temple. Pushing against them with both hands, he prayed, "Let me die with the Philistines." And the temple crashed down.

Judges 16:29–30

Do you have a favorite superhero? There are so many to choose from—Superman, Batman, Spiderman, and Daredevil are just a few. Samson is not just a superhero. He carried out many heroic acts for Israel's freedom. God's Spirit was with him from beginning to end. He tore a lion apart with his bare hands! He killed a thousand men using a donkey's jawbone! He tore the gates off the city of Gaza! By the power of the Spirit, Samson did many amazing things for Israel.

The greatest thing Samson did was the

last thing he ever did. Samson's enemies had captured him and cut out his eyes. He was on display like an animal in a zoo. Had his heroic life ended in defeat?

Samson was taken into a temple to entertain his enemies. Three thousand men and women were watching. He put his hands on the pillars that held the roof of the building. "O God, please strengthen me one more time," Samson prayed. Then God enabled him to push over the pillars, and this destroyed the temple. Thousands of enemies died with Samson that day.

Samson did this to show one last time that God was with him. He died for God's people, and this makes him much more than a super-hero. Samson is a hero of the faith.

Dear God, help me to be a hero of the faith like Samson. Amen.

"...the glory of God."

The heavens proclaim the glory of God. The skies display his craftsmanship. Day after day they continue to speak; night after night they make him known.

Psalm 19:1–2

Do you want to know God? Is there someone you love who you hope will believe in God? Here is an easy way to see God. The heavens announce God's glory. The skies shout about the work of His hands.

This has been happening since the fourth day of Creation, when God said, "Let bright lights appear in the sky." Since then, they continue to speak about God day after day. Night after night, they make Him known. If only people would pay attention! It doesn't matter where you are from or what language you speak. Nature tells all about God. Yes, God is invisible. But the Bible says that God and all of His power can be seen through nature.

Many people pray that their family and friends will be open to God. They want them to believe in Jesus Christ. We hope they will hear the gospel. God's Creation is the greatest preacher of all. Let's pray that everyone will see it and believe it!

Dear God, help me to open my eyes every day to see Your wonderful creation. Amen.

"There is the lamb of God."

The next day John saw Jesus coming toward him and said, "Look! There is the Lamb of God who takes away the sin of the world!"

JOHN 1:29

Everyone knows that Jesus wasn't really a lamb. He was a man. For His whole life, He wasn't like a lamb at all. He was strong and bold until the end. Then He became like a lamb. The Bible says that when Jesus died, "He was led as a lamb to the slaughter. And as a sheep is silent before the shearers, he did not open his mouth."

In the times of the Old Testament, people made sacrifices to God for their sins. These sacrifices were usually lambs. Year after year, people made these sacrifices. Then Jesus came. He was the last sacrifice for sin. No one has to kill a little lamb again because of sin. Jesus is the Lamb of God whose death took away the sin of the world. "For God so loved the world that he gave his only Son, so that everyone who believes in him will not perish but have eternal life."

Dear God, thank You for giving Jesus to be the sacrifice for my sin. Amen.

"Please give me a drink."

Jesus, tired from the long walk, sat wearily beside the well about noontime. Soon a Samaritan woman came to draw water, and Jesus said to her, "Please give me a drink."
JOHN 4:6–7

It was about noon one day, and Jesus was alone, resting by a well. A woman came to the well to draw out some water. Jesus asked her to give Him some. In those days, this wasn't done. Men and women had nothing to do with each other unless they were married. Plus, the woman in this story was a Samaritan. Jesus was a Jew. The Jews thought they were much better than the Samaritans, and so they never spoke to each other.

Most women in those days got their water in the morning. Then they had what they needed for that day. Plus, they didn't have to carry water in the heat of the day. But this woman was an outcast in her village. She had been married several times. The other women stayed away from her because she was a sinner.

You might say this woman had three strikes against her. She was a sinner. She was a Samaritan. She was a woman. To everyone else, she was out, but not to Jesus. This story shows that Jesus came for the outcasts of this world. He came for sinners and poor people. He came for everyone, no matter who they are.

Dear God, thank You for not playing favorites—You care for everyone. Amen.

"...the peace that comes from Christ."

And let the peace that comes from Christ rule in your hearts. For as members of one body you are all called to live in peace. And always be thankful.

COLOSSIANS 3:15

Jesus said, "I am leaving you with a gift—peace of mind and heart. And the peace I give isn't like the peace the world gives. So don't be troubled or afraid."

Ever since the times of Jesus, peace has been compared with a dove. This bird is also a symbol of the Holy Spirit. When the Spirit came down upon Jesus, it looked like a dove. The Holy Spirit gives us God's peace.

Because Christians have God's Spirit, we don't worry about anything. Instead, we pray about everything. In prayer, we tell God what we need, and we thank Him for all things. This brings us God's peace. This peace is impossible to explain. It is far more wonderful than your mind can understand. Let this peace guard your heart and mind as you live in Christ.

Doves are very shy. It is easy to scare them away. This is true with peace, too. It can come and go like a bird. One day, Jesus will bring His peace to the earth to stay forever. He will bring the kingdom of peace.

Dear God, I thank You that one day You'll bring peace to the earth.
Amen.

Dear God, thank You for Your Word and the important lessons we can learn from it! Amen.